PERSONAL FINANCE MANAGEMENT

Mastering The Art of Budgeting

KELLY STEWART

Copyright Page

Copyright © 2023 by KELLY STEWART

Part 4. Investments

Part 1

This foundational chapter introduces the concept of personal finance, emphasizing its significance in achieving financial well-being and security. By grasping the fundamental principles of personal finance, readers will be better equipped to make informed financial decisions that positively impact their lives.

Section 1: What is Personal Finance?

Defining Personal Finance
- Personal finance involves managing money, setting financial goals, and making prudent financial decisions.
- Understanding how personal finance applies to individuals' income, expenses, savings, and investments.

Importance of Personal Finance
- Highlighting the role of personal finance in achieving financial goals and building wealth over time.
- Emphasizing the connection between financial choices and overall life satisfaction.

Section 2: Financial Goals and Budgeting

Setting Financial Goals
- The significance of clear and achievable financial goals, such as saving for retirement, buying a home, or funding education.
- Identifying short-term and long-term goals and their role in guiding financial decisions.

Budgeting Basics
- Introducing the concept of budgeting as a tool to manage income and expenses.
- Creating a budget to track spending, prioritize expenses, and achieve financial goals.

Section 3: Managing Debt and Credit

Understanding Debt
- Differentiating between good and bad debt and the potential impact of excessive debt on financial well-being.
- Exploring common types of debt, such as credit card debt, student loans, and mortgages.

Credit and Credit Scores
- Defining credit and its importance in borrowing money and making major purchases.
- Explaining credit scores, how they are calculated, and their impact on borrowing costs.

Section 4: Building Savings and Investments

The Importance of Saving
- Exploring the value of saving money for emergencies, future expenses, and long-term goals.
- Emphasizing the habit of saving as a foundation for financial security.

Investment Basics
- Introducing the concept of investing as a means to grow wealth over time.
- Differentiating between savings and investments and understanding risk and return.

Section 5: Personal Finance Mindset

Financial Literacy
- Stressing the importance of educating oneself about personal finance concepts, terminology, and strategies.
- The benefits of making informed financial decisions and avoiding common pitfalls.

Financial Decision-Making
- Encouraging thoughtful decision-making based on individual circumstances, values, and goals.
- Discussing the influence of emotions and behavioral biases on financial choices.

You can establish the foundation for a comprehensive understanding of personal finance by thoroughly studying the information provided in this chapter. With this information, you'll be better equipped to manage your finances, make wise choices, and strive toward your financial goals.

Section 1: The Role of Career Planning

Defining Career Planning
- Career planning involves setting career goals, developing skills, and making decisions that lead to professional growth and advancement.
- Understanding how career choices impact income, job satisfaction, and overall well-being.

Career and Financial Success
- Exploring the relationship between career progression and financial stability.
- Emphasizing how career decisions influence earning potential and long-term financial goals.

Section 2: Self-Assessment and Goal Setting

Self-Assessment
- Evaluating personal strengths, skills, interests, and values to determine suitable career paths.

- Identifying transferable skills and areas for improvement.

Setting Career Goals
- Establishing short-term and long-term career goals aligned with personal aspirations.
- Defining goals related to job titles, salaries, job satisfaction, and work-life balance.

Section 3: Exploring Career Options

Researching Industries and Occupations
- Conducting research to understand the job market, demand for specific skills, and potential growth industries.
- Utilizing online resources, networking, and informational interviews to gather information.

Education and Skill Development
- Identifying the education, training, and certifications required for different career paths.
- Discussing the importance of continuous learning and skill development in a rapidly changing job market.

Section 4: Navigating Career Transitions

Job Changes and Advancement
- Exploring strategies for advancing within a current job or transitioning to a new role.
- The significance of building a strong professional network and seeking mentorship.

Entrepreneurship and Freelancing
- Considering the option of starting a business or working as a freelancer.
- Understanding the challenges and rewards of entrepreneurship and self-employment.

Section 5: Balancing Career and Life

Work-Life Balance
- Highlighting the importance of maintaining a healthy work-life balance for overall well-being.
- Time management, boundary-setting, and self-care prioritization techniques.

Personal Fulfillment
- Recognizing the role of personal fulfillment in career satisfaction and overall happiness.
- Aligning career choices with personal values and passions.

You'll obtain a full understanding of career planning and its impact on your financial path if you immerse yourself in the intricacies described in this chapter. This knowledge will enable you to make sensible career decisions, set meaningful goals, and move toward professional and financial success.

Section 1: Understanding Financial Statements

Balance Sheet
- Defining the balance sheet as a snapshot of an individual's financial position, detailing assets, liabilities, and net worth.
- Exploring how the balance sheet reflects financial stability and solvency.

Income Statement
- Explaining the income statement as a record of income and expenses over a specific period.
- Understanding how the income statement reflects cash flow and financial performance.

Section 2: Financial Tools and Resources

Personal Financial Software
- Introducing financial software and apps that help track income, expenses, and net worth.

- Discussing the benefits of using technology to manage personal finances.

Financial Ratios
- Exploring key financial ratios that assess an individual's financial health, such as debt-to-income ratio and savings rate.
- Understanding how ratios provide insights into financial well-being.
-

Section 3: Budgeting Basics

Importance of Budgeting
- Emphasizing budgeting as a tool for managing income, expenses, and achieving financial goals.
- Highlighting the role of budgeting in preventing overspending and fostering financial discipline.

Creating a Budget
- Step-by-step guide to creating a budget, including tracking income, categorizing expenses, and setting spending limits.
- Exploring the envelope method, zero-based budgeting, and 50/30/20 budgeting.

Section 4: Emergency Funds and Savings Goals

Emergency Funds
- Defining emergency funds as a critical financial safety net for unexpected expenses.
- Discussing the recommended size of emergency funds and where to keep them.

Savings Goals
- Setting and prioritizing savings goals for short-term and long-term needs.
- Exploring saving strategies for specific goals such as buying a home, funding education, and retirement.

Section 5: Financial Tracking and Adjustments

Regular Financial Check-Ins
- Emphasizing the importance of regularly reviewing financial statements, budgets, and goals.
- Making necessary adjustments to align with changing circumstances.

Financial Goals Reassessment

- Exploring how life changes can impact financial goals and priorities.
- The need to adapt budgets and savings strategies accordingly.

You will develop a full understanding of financial statements, tools, and budgeting by immersing yourself in the intricacies presented in this chapter. This information will enable you to assess your financial health, efficiently use financial tools, and develop a budget that meets your financial objectives and aspirations.

Part 2. Money Management

Chapter 4. Managing Income Taxes

For your financial condition to be optimized, it's crucial to comprehend and manage income taxes. This chapter goes deeply into the complexities of income taxes, offering information on various tax structures, tax-planning techniques, and ways to reduce your tax bill.

Section 1: Types of Taxes

Income Taxes
- Understanding the progressive nature of income taxes based on different income levels.
- How income taxes are calculated and the importance of accurate reporting.

Capital Gains Taxes
- Exploring taxes on profits made from selling investments or assets.
- Identifying the differences in tax rates for short- and long-term capital gains.

Social Security and Medicare Taxes
- Understanding payroll taxes for funding Social Security and Medicare programs.
- Examining the current tax rates and how they impact your earnings.

Tax-Advantaged Accounts
- Exploring retirement accounts like 401(k)s and IRAs that offer tax benefits.
- How contributions to these accounts can reduce your taxable income.

Tax Deductions and Credits
- Identifying deductible expenses that can lower your taxable income.
- Exploring tax credits for education, childcare, and energy-efficient home improvements.

Tax-Efficient Investing
- Recognizing how taxes affect investment returns.
- Strategies for minimizing taxes on investment gains and distributions.

Section 3: Minimizing Tax Liability

Year-Round Tax Planning
- Planning throughout the year to optimize your tax situation.
- Estimated tax payments and avoiding penalties for underpayment.

Tax Filing Strategies
- Deciding between standard deduction and itemizing deductions.
- Exploring strategies for maximizing deductions and credits.

Professional Tax Advice
- The benefits of consulting with tax professionals, accountants, or financial advisors.
- How experts can help you navigate complex tax codes and identify potential savings.

You'll develop a thorough understanding of handling income taxes if you thoroughly absorb the information provided in this chapter. Your ability to organize your money strategically, make informed decisions, and reduce your tax liability while adhering to the law will all be facilitated by this information.

Chapter 5. Managing Checking and Savings Accounts

Effectively managing your checking and savings accounts is fundamental to keeping financial stability and achieving your financial goals. This chapter offers a comprehensive guide to understanding these important bank accounts and maximizing their benefits.

Section 1: Types of Bank Accounts

Checking Accounts
- Definition and purpose of checking accounts
- Features like debit cards, check-writing, and online banking
- How to choose a checking account that suits your needs

Savings Accounts
- Introduction to savings accounts and their role in financial planning
- Interest rates and compounding for savings growth
- Exploring different types of savings accounts and their benefits

Section 2: Managing and Balancing Accounts

Keeping Track of Transactions
- Monitoring account activity through statements and online banking
- Recording deposits, withdrawals, and transfers accurately
- Detecting and resolving any discrepancies promptly

Preventing Overdrafts and Fees
- Understanding overdraft protection options
- Strategies to avoid overdrafts and associated fees
- The importance of maintaining a buffer in your account

Leveraging Online Tools
- Utilizing online and mobile banking apps
- Setting up account alerts for balance changes and transactions
- Transferring funds and managing accounts conveniently

Section 3: Savings Strategies and Goals

Setting Savings Goals
- Defining short-term and long-term savings objectives.
- Allocating funds for emergencies, travel, education, and more.
- Creating a savings plan that aligns with your financial aspirations

Automating Savings Contributions.
- The benefits of setting up automatic transfers
- Ensuring consistent savings without the need for manual intervention
- Utilizing direct deposits for effortless savings allocation

Building an Emergency Fund
- Understanding the importance of an emergency fund
- Calculating the ideal size of your emergency fund
- Using savings accounts for easy access to emergency funds

By immersing yourself in the details described within this chapter, you'll gain a comprehensive understanding of checking and savings accounts. This information will empower you to effectively manage your funds, avoid unnecessary fees, and work toward your savings goals.

Chapter 6. Building and Maintaining Good Credit

A strong credit history is essential for various financial opportunities and goals. This chapter delves into the intricacies of building and maintaining good credit, ensuring that you can access favorable lending terms and make informed financial decisions.

Section 1: Importance of Credit Scores

Understanding Credit Scores
- Definition and components of a credit score
- The significance of credit scores in borrowing and financial transactions
- How credit scores are used by lenders, landlords, and employers

Factors Affecting Credit Scores
- Payment history, credit utilization, length of credit history, and more
- The impact of credit inquiries and recent credit activity
- Strategies for positively influencing credit score factors

Section 2: Building Positive Credit History

Starting with a Credit History
- Initiating your credit history if you're new to borrowing
- Secured credit cards and credit-building loans
- Establishing a solid foundation for your credit profile

Responsible Credit Card Usage
- Guidelines for using credit cards effectively
- Keeping credit card balances low and manageable
- Consistently paying credit card bills on time

Diversifying Credit Types
- Exploring different types of credit accounts (credit cards, installment loans)
- The benefits of having a mix of credit types in your history
- Avoiding overextending yourself with excessive credit accounts

Section 3: Credit Reports and Monitoring

Requesting and Reviewing Credit Reports
- The importance of obtaining and reviewing your credit reports
- How to request free annual credit reports from major credit bureaus
- Checking for inaccuracies, errors, and signs of identity theft

Regular Credit Monitoring
- Utilizing credit monitoring services for ongoing awareness
- Staying vigilant against suspicious or unauthorized activity
- Identifying changes in your credit report and score over time

Section 4: Handling Credit Challenges

Addressing Negative Credit Events
- Strategies for recovering from missed payments or defaults
- Rebuilding credit after financial setbacks
- Negotiating with creditors and seeking credit counseling if needed

Avoiding Credit Pitfalls

- Recognizing common credit mistakes and pitfalls
- The dangers of maxing out credit cards and relying on credit for daily expenses
- Making informed decisions to prevent credit troubles

By immersing yourself in the details outlined within this chapter, you'll gain a comprehensive understanding of credit management. This knowledge will empower you to build and maintain a strong credit profile, unlock favorable lending terms, and navigate financial opportunities with confidence.

Credit cards and consumer loans are important financial tools that can provide convenience and flexibility when managed responsibly. This chapter delves into the intricacies of using credit cards and obtaining consumer loans while emphasizing the significance of responsible borrowing.

Section 1: Credit Card Essentials

Understanding Credit Cards
- Definition and purpose of credit cards
- How credit card transactions work
- Available credit limits and utilization rates

Types of Credit Cards
- Rewards cards: cash back, travel rewards, and points
- Secured credit cards for credit building or rebuilding
- Specialty cards tailored to specific needs

Responsible Credit Card Usage
- Advantages of paying down credit card bills completely
- Managing monthly credit card statements and due dates
- Avoiding late payments and associated fees

Managing Credit Card Balances
- Calculating and understanding interest rates (APR)
- Strategies for paying off credit card debt
- Minimizing interest payments through timely payments

Section 2: Consumer Loans

Types of Consumer Loans
- Personal loans for various needs: debt consolidation, medical expenses, etc.
- Auto loans for purchasing vehicles
- Student loans for education-related expenses

Factors Influencing Loan Terms
- Credit scores and their impact on loan approvals and interest rates
- Loan term (duration) and its effects on monthly payments

- The significance of comparing loan offers from several lenders

Loan Application and Approval Process
- Required documentation for loan applications
- Prequalification vs. preapproval for loans
- Reviewing loan terms, fees, and associated costs

Loan Repayment Strategies
- Setting a repayment plan that aligns with your budget
- Exploring options for accelerated loan repayment
- Avoiding penalties for early loan repayment

Section 3: Responsible Borrowing Practices

Balancing Debt and Financial Goals
- Evaluating your financial situation before taking on debt
- Borrow only what you can afford to repay
- Weighing the benefits and costs of borrowing

Building and Maintaining Good Credit
- The role of loans and credit cards in building credit history
- Strategies for using credit to strengthen your credit profile
- The impact of missed payments and late repayments on credit scores

Avoiding Predatory Lending
- Identifying red flags of predatory lending practices
- How to recognize and avoid high-interest loans and hidden fees
- Seeking reputable lenders with transparent terms

By delving into the details outlined in this chapter, you'll gain a comprehensive understanding of credit cards and consumer loans. Armed with this knowledge, you'll be able to make informed borrowing decisions, use credit responsibly, and manage debt effectively to achieve your financial goals.

Chapter 8. Vehicles and Other Major Purchases

Making major purchases, such as a vehicle or other significant items, requires careful planning and consideration. This chapter provides a comprehensive guide to navigating the process of making substantial purchases, ensuring that you make informed decisions that align with your financial goals.

Section 1: Planning Major Purchases

Assessing Your Needs and Budget
- Identifying the purpose and necessity of the purchase
- Setting a budget that factors in the full cost of ownership
- Balancing immediate desires with long-term financial goals

Researching Options
- Gathering information about available products or services
- Reading reviews, comparing features, and evaluating alternatives
- Determining the most suitable option based on your needs

Evaluating Affordability
- Understanding the total cost of the purchase, including taxes and fees
- Factoring in ongoing expenses, maintenance, and insurance
- Ensuring that the purchase fits comfortably within your budget

Section 2: Financing and Loans

Understanding Financing Options
- Exploring financing options provided by dealerships and banks
- Assessing the pros and cons of different financing methods
- Determining whether financing or paying upfront is more suitable

Loan Terms and Interest Rates
- Reading and comprehending loan agreements
- Loan terms and interest rates are negotiated with lenders.
- Calculating the overall cost of borrowing, including interest payments

Dealing with Dealerships
- Navigating the negotiation process with dealers
- Being prepared to walk away if terms are unfavorable
- Understanding dealer add-ons and additional costs

Section 3: Avoiding Common Pitfalls

Thorough Inspection and Due Diligence
- Inspecting vehicles or items before finalizing the purchase
- Verifying the condition and history of used products
- Avoiding impulse purchases and rushed decisions

Warranty and Return Policies
- Understanding warranty coverage and limitations
- Inquiring about return policies and satisfaction guarantees
- Protecting your consumer rights and ensuring recourse if issues arise

Additional Costs and Considerations

- Factoring in insurance costs and potential fluctuations in premiums
- Planning for maintenance and repairs over the product's lifespan
- Exploring resale value and potential depreciation

By immersing yourself in the facts presented inside this chapter, you'll obtain a full understanding of how to approach significant purchases wisely and safely. Armed with this knowledge, you'll be better prepared to make informed judgments, avoid frequent mistakes, and ensure that your purchases align with your financial well-being.

Securing suitable and affordable housing is a significant financial decision that impacts your long-term financial stability. This chapter provides a thorough exploration of housing options, considerations, and strategies to ensure you make informed choices that align with your financial goals.

Section 1: Housing Options

Renting vs. Buying
- Weighing the advantages and disadvantages of renting and homeownership
- Considering factors like financial flexibility, maintenance, and long-term plans
- Assessing which option best suits your current and future needs

Types of Housing
- Exploring different housing arrangements: apartments, condos, houses
- Understanding the implications of each housing type on costs and lifestyle

- Evaluating factors such as location, amenities, and community features

Section 2: Homeownership Preparation

Financial Readiness for Homeownership
- Evaluating your financial situation and readiness to become a homeowner
- Assessing your credit score and financial stability for mortgage approval
- Calculating how much you can afford based on your income and debt

Mortgage Options and Affordability
- Understanding the types of mortgages available (fixed, adjustable, etc.)
- Exploring mortgage terms and their impact on monthly payments
- Determining an affordable monthly mortgage payment within your budget

Section 3: Navigating the Homebuying Process

Research and House Hunting
- Researching neighborhoods, schools, and local amenities
- Attending open houses, tours, and engaging with real estate agents

- Identifying must-have features and prioritizing preferences

Making an Offer and Negotiating
- Crafting a competitive offer that considers market trends and property value
- Negotiating terms with the seller, including price and contingencies
- Understanding the importance of property inspections and due diligence

Understanding Home Expenses
- Estimating ongoing homeownership costs beyond the mortgage
- Budgeting for property taxes, insurance, utilities, and maintenance
- Planning for unexpected repairs and emergencies

Section 4: Financial Benefits and Challenges

Equity Building Through Homeownership
- Understanding how homeownership builds equity over time
- The potential for appreciation and long-term financial benefits

- Considering the home as an investment for your financial future

Potential Risks and Pitfalls
- Recognizing the potential downsides of homeownership, such as market volatility,
- Avoiding common mistakes, like overextending financially
- Being prepared for unexpected expenses and financial fluctuations

By immersing yourself in the facts presented within this chapter, you'll build a full awareness of housing possibilities, the homebuying process, and the financial ramifications of getting inexpensive housing. This knowledge will empower you to make informed decisions that support your financial well-being and long-term stability.

Part 3. Income and Asset Protection

Chapter 10. Managing Property and Liability Risk

Effectively managing property and liability risks is vital for maintaining your assets and financial well-being. This chapter digs into the intricacies of understanding and minimizing these risks through insurance and smart decision-making.

Section 1: Understanding Property and Liability Risk

Property Risk
- Defining property risk and its potential sources (natural disasters, theft, etc.)
- The financial impact of property damage, loss, or destruction
- Identifying measures to reduce property risk, such as preventive maintenance

Liability Risk
- Exploring liability risk in personal and professional contexts
- The potential legal and financial consequences of liability claims

- Strategies for minimizing liability risk through careful behavior and communication

Section 2: Property Insurance

Types of Property Insurance
- Homeowners insurance: coverage for property damage, theft, and liability
- Renters insurance: protection for personal belongings and liability
- Condo insurance: tailored coverage for condominium owners
- Evaluating which type of property insurance aligns with your living situation

Coverage Options and Limits
- Exploring the different coverage options within property insurance
- Determining appropriate coverage limits based on your assets and needs
- Balancing comprehensive coverage with affordability

Claims Process
- Navigating the steps to file a property insurance claim

- Documenting and providing evidence of property damage or loss
- Understanding how the claims process leads to compensation

Section 3: Liability Insurance

Importance of Liability Coverage
- Understanding the role of liability insurance in personal protection
- Auto liability insurance: coverage for accidents and injuries
- Personal liability insurance: protection against legal claims

Types of Liability Insurance
- Auto liability insurance: mandatory coverage for drivers
- Personal liability insurance: coverage for legal claims on personal property
- Exploring additional types of liability insurance, such as umbrella policies

Safeguarding Against Legal and Financial Consequences
- Recognizing the potential costs of legal disputes and liabilities
- Using liability insurance to cover legal defense and settlement costs

- How liability insurance supports your financial stability and peace of mind

By immersing yourself in the details outlined within this chapter, you'll gain a comprehensive understanding of property and liability risks and how to manage them effectively. This knowledge will empower you to make informed decisions, protect your assets, and navigate unforeseen challenges with confidence.

As healthcare costs continue to rise, proactive planning is essential to ensure your financial well-being in the face of medical expenses. This chapter offers a comprehensive guide to understanding healthcare expenses, exploring insurance options, and creating a plan to manage these costs.

Section 1: Understanding Health Care Costs

The Rising Costs of Medical Care
- Examining the factors contributing to the escalating costs of healthcare
- The potential impact of high medical expenses on your finances
- The importance of financial preparedness to cover health care needs

Common Health Care Expenses
- Identifying typical health care costs (premiums, deductibles, co-pays)
- Understanding out-of-pocket expenses and their variability

- Budgeting for prescription medications, medical procedures, and preventive care

Section 2: Health Insurance Basics

Different Types of Health Insurance Plans
- Preferred Provider Organization (PPO), Health Maintenance Organization (HMO), etc.
- The varying levels of coverage and flexibility offered by different plans
- Evaluating which health insurance plan aligns with your health needs and financial situation

Evaluating Health Insurance Coverage
- Understanding the benefits and limitations of your chosen health insurance plan
- Exploring coverage for medical services, prescription drugs, specialists, and more
- Reviewing the network of health care providers and facilities covered by your plan

Guidelines for Your Health Insurance Policy
- Reading and comprehending the fine print of your insurance policy

- Understanding terms like co-insurance, co-payment, and annual out-of-pocket maximum
- Ensuring that you're aware of any preauthorization requirements and limitations

Section 3: Flexible Spending Accounts and Health Savings Accounts

Benefits of Tax-Advantaged Health Care Accounts
- The advantages of HSAs and FSAs for managing health care costs
- How these accounts offer tax benefits and reduce your taxable income
- Maximizing the potential of HSAs and FSAs to save on health care expenses

How HSAs and FSAs Work
- Eligibility requirements and contribution limits for HSAs and FSAs
- Using HSAs for qualified medical expenses and potential long-term savings
- Utilizing FSAs to cover eligible health care costs through pre-tax contributions

You will get a thorough awareness of health care prices, insurance options, and methods for managing your medical bills by thoroughly studying the information provided in this chapter. With this information, you'll be better equipped to confidently navigate the complicated world of health care and secure your financial security in the event of medical emergencies.

A strong instrument for minimizing financial risk and safeguarding your assets and loved ones is insurance. This chapter goes further into insurance planning, guiding you through the various insurance options and how to develop a comprehensive coverage strategy.

Section 1: Understanding the Role of Insurance

Purpose of Insurance
- Defining the concept of insurance and its purpose in financial planning
- How insurance transfers the risk of financial loss from individuals to insurers
- The peace of mind and security that insurance provides

Types of Insurance
- Introduction to various types of insurance (life, health, auto, home, etc.)
- Understanding the specific risks each type of insurance addresses
- Exploring the range of coverage options available to individuals

Section 2: Life Insurance

Determining Coverage Needs
- Identifying the purpose of life insurance: income replacement, debt coverage, etc.
- Calculating the appropriate coverage amount based on financial responsibilities
- Factoring in outstanding debts, future expenses, and long-term financial goals

Types of Life Insurance Policies
- Term life insurance: temporary coverage for a specific period
- Whole life insurance: permanent coverage with cash value accumulation
- Universal life insurance: flexible coverage with investment components

Beneficiaries and Payout Process
- Naming beneficiaries and understanding their role in the policy
- How the life insurance payout process works
- The importance of keeping beneficiary information up to date

Section 3: Disability and Long-Term Care Insurance

Protecting Against Income Loss
- Recognizing the importance of income protection in cases of disability
- Understanding the financial impact of disability on your ability to earn
- How disability insurance provides a safety net during periods of inability to work

Long-Term Care Insurance
- The significance of planning for potential long-term care needs
- Long-term care insurance covers expenses related to extended care
- Exploring the benefits of long-term care insurance for aging individuals

Section 4: Estate Planning and Insurance

Incorporating Insurance into Estate Planning
- The role of insurance in providing for loved ones after your passing
- Ensuring financial stability for beneficiaries in the event of your death

- Coordinating insurance coverage with wills, trusts, and other estate planning tools

Ensuring Financial Security for Loved Ones
- Addressing the financial needs of dependents and family members
- How insurance can replace lost income, cover debts, and provide for education
- Creating a comprehensive estate plan that includes insurance considerations

You will gain a full understanding of insurance planning by immersing yourself in the intricacies presented in this chapter. This understanding will enable you to design a customized insurance policy that safeguards your assets, reduces financial risks, and provides for your loved ones in times of need.

Part 4. Investments

Chapter 13. Investment Fundamentals

Understanding the core principles of investing is crucial for building wealth and achieving your financial goals. This chapter provides an in-depth exploration of investment fundamentals, including risk, return, types of investments, and strategies for making informed investment decisions.

Section 1: Understanding Investments

Defining Investments
- Investments involve putting money into assets with the goal of generating returns over time.
- Investments range from stocks and bonds to real estate and alternative investments.

Savings vs. Investing
- Distinguishing between saving money in low-risk accounts and investing for potential higher returns.
- Exploring the trade-offs between liquidity and earning potential.

Setting Investment Goals
- Identifying short-term and long-term financial objectives.
- Aligning investment strategies with personal goals, such as retirement, education, or purchasing a home.

Section 2: Risk and Return

Risk and Reward Relationship
- Understanding the principle that higher potential returns are usually accompanied by higher levels of risk.
- The importance of evaluating your risk tolerance before making investment decisions.

Assessing Risk Tolerance
- Evaluating your ability to withstand investment losses without jeopardizing your financial well-being.
- Considering factors like time horizon, financial obligations, and emotional comfort with risk.

Diversification

- Exploring the strategy of spreading investments across different assets to mitigate risk.
- Reducing the impact of poor performance in one investment through a diversified portfolio.

Section 3: Types of Investments

Stocks

- Stocks represent ownership in a company and offer potential for capital appreciation and dividends.
- Differentiating between common and preferred stocks and understanding their characteristics.

Bonds

- Bonds are debt securities issued by governments or corporations to raise capital.
- Exploring the relationship between bond prices, interest rates, and fixed income.

Mutual Funds and Exchange-Traded Funds (ETFs)

- Mutual funds pool money from multiple investors to invest in a diversified portfolio.
- ETFs are similar to mutual funds but trade on stock exchanges like individual stocks.

Section 4: Strategies for Informed Investing

Long-Term Perspective

- Understanding the benefits of a long-term investment horizon.
- Harnessing the power of compounding to grow wealth over time.

Research and Due Diligence

- Conducting thorough research before making investment decisions.
- Evaluating historical performance, fund managers, and economic trends.

Asset Allocation

- Allocating your investment portfolio across different asset classes (stocks, bonds, etc.).
- Balancing risk and return through strategic diversification.

By immersing yourself in the details outlined within this chapter, you'll gain a comprehensive understanding of investment fundamentals. This knowledge will empower you to make informed investment choices, navigate market fluctuations, and work towards achieving your financial aspirations.

CHAPTER 14. Investing in Stocks and Bonds

Investing in stocks and bonds is a cornerstone of building a diversified investment portfolio. This chapter delves deeper into the intricacies of these two asset classes, providing insights into their characteristics, benefits, and strategies for successful investment.

Section 1: Stock Market Basics

Understanding Stocks
- Stocks represent ownership shares in a company, entitling investors to a portion of its profits and losses.
- Stocks are traded on stock exchanges, where prices fluctuate based on supply and demand.

Factors Influencing Stock Prices
- Stock prices are influenced by factors such as company performance, industry trends, and economic conditions.
- External events, news, and investor sentiment also impact stock prices.

Types of Stocks
- Common stocks: Offer ownership and voting rights in the company.
- Preferred stocks: Provide fixed dividends and priority in receiving company assets in case of bankruptcy.

Section 2: Bonds and Fixed-Income Investments

Understanding Bonds
- Bonds are debt securities issued by governments, municipalities, or corporations to raise capital.
- Bondholders receive regular interest payments (coupon payments) and the principal amount upon maturity.

Interest Rates and Bond Prices
- The inverse relationship between interest rates and bond prices: when interest rates rise, bond prices fall, and vice versa.
- How changes in interest rates affect the yield and value of existing bonds.

Building a Stock and Bond Portfolio

Asset Allocation
- Allocating your investment portfolio between stocks and bonds based on your risk tolerance and financial goals.
- Balancing potential returns with risk management through diversification.

Risk Management
- How combining stocks and bonds in a portfolio can help reduce overall portfolio volatility.
- Using bonds as a stabilizing force during market downturns.

Investment Horizon
- Considering your investment horizon when deciding on the allocation between stocks and bonds.
- Short-term goals may favor bonds, while long-term goals may involve a higher allocation to stocks.

Section 3: Strategies for Successful Investing

Research and Fundamental Analysis
- Conducting thorough research on individual companies before investing in their stocks.
- Analyzing financial statements, competitive landscape, and growth potential.

Dollar-Cost Averaging
- Investing a fixed amount at regular intervals regardless of market conditions.
- Reducing the impact of market volatility on your investment returns.

Rebalancing Your Portfolio
- Regularly reviewing and adjusting your portfolio to maintain the desired asset allocation.
- Selling overperforming assets and buying underperforming ones to bring the portfolio back in line.

By immersing yourself in the details outlined in this chapter, you'll gain a comprehensive understanding of investing in stocks and bonds. This knowledge will empower you to make informed investment decisions, construct a balanced portfolio, and work towards achieving your financial objectives.

Chapter 15. Investing Through Mutual Funds

Investing through mutual funds offers a convenient and diversified approach to building wealth. This chapter delves deeper into the world of mutual funds, providing insights into their benefits, types, and strategies for maximizing their potential.

Section 1: Introduction to Mutual Funds

Defining Mutual Funds
- Mutual funds pool money from multiple investors to invest in a diversified portfolio of assets.
- Professional fund managers make investment decisions on behalf of fund investors.

Benefits of Mutual Funds
- Diversification: Investing in a range of assets to spread risk.
- Professional Management: Experienced fund managers oversee investment decisions.
- Accessibility: Common assets are effectively open for individual financial backers.

Mutual Fund Structure
- Open-End Funds: Unlimited shares issued, bought, and sold at net asset value (NAV).
- Closed-End Funds: Limited shares issued through an initial public offering (IPO), traded on exchanges.

Section 2: Types of Mutual Funds

Equity Funds
- Invest primarily in stocks of various companies across industries and sectors.
- Categories include large-cap, mid-cap, small-cap, and international equity funds.

Bond Funds
- Focus on investing in bonds issued by governments or corporations.
- Types incorporate government securities, corporate securities, and civil securities.

Hybrid Funds

- Blend both stocks and bonds in varying proportions to achieve a balance of growth and income.
- Designed for investors seeking moderate risk and return profiles.

Section 3: Strategies for Investing with Mutual Funds

Systematic Investment Plans (SIPs)

- Contribute a proper sum consistently, advancing restrained financial planning.
- Reduces the impact of market volatility and promotes long-term wealth accumulation.

Choosing the Right Fund

- Assessing your risk tolerance, investment goals, and time horizon.
- Researching fund performance, expense ratios, and fund managers' track records.

Managing and Monitoring Funds

- Regularly review fund performance and portfolio composition.

- Adjust your investment strategy based on changing goals and market conditions.

Managing Fees and Expenses
- Analyzing expense ratios and fees associated with the mutual fund.
- Opting for low-cost index funds to maximize returns.

By submerging yourself in the subtleties illustrated inside this section, you'll acquire an exhaustive comprehension of effective money management through shared reserves. This information will enable you to pick the right assets, build a broadened portfolio, and influence the advantages of expert administration in quest for your monetary objectives.

Chapter 16. Real Estate and High-Risk Investments

This section dives into the universe of land effective money management and high-risk ventures, giving experiences into their possible prizes, dangers, and procedures for moving toward these novel speculation valuable open doors.

Section 1: Investing in Real Estate

Real Estate as an Investment
- Land offers the potential for rental pay, property appreciation, and tax cuts.
- Exploring the role of real estate in diversifying an investment portfolio.

Types of Real Estate Investments
- Direct Ownership: Purchasing property to rent, sell, or generate income.
- Real Estate Investment Trusts (REITs): Investing in a portfolio of real estate assets through publicly traded stocks.

Risks and Rewards
- Property management challenges, vacancy risks, and property value fluctuations.
- Long-term potential for passive income and capital appreciation.

Section 2: High-Risk Investments

Understanding High-Risk Investments
- High-risk investments involve substantial potential returns but come with elevated levels of risk.
- Examples include venture capital, cryptocurrencies, and speculative stocks.

Venture Capital and Startups
- Investing in early-stage companies with high growth potential.
- The potential for significant returns but also high failure rates.

Cryptocurrencies and Alternative Investments
- Exploring the world of cryptocurrencies like Bitcoin and Ethereum.
- Understanding the speculative nature and volatility of these investments.

Section 3: Strategies for Navigating High-Risk Investments

Thorough Research and Due Diligence
- Investigating the fundamentals, market trends, and potential risks of high-risk investments.
- Consulting experts and seeking credible sources of information.

Risk Management
- Allocating only a small portion of your portfolio to high-risk investments.
- Setting clear risk limits to prevent overexposure.

Long-Term Perspective
- Acknowledging that high-risk investments can be volatile in the short term.
- Aiming for a long-term horizon to potentially benefit from market trends.

Avoiding Emotional Decision-Making
- Making investment decisions based on data and analysis rather than emotions.
- Being prepared for the possibility of losses and avoiding impulsive actions.

By immersing yourself in the details outlined within this chapter, you will gain a comprehensive understanding of real estate investing and high- threat investments. This knowledge will empower you to make informed opinions, manage pitfalls effectively, and explore openings that align with your threat forbearance and investment pretensions.

This chapter focuses on the critical aspects of retirement planning and estate planning, helping you secure your financial future and ensure a smooth transition of assets to your heirs.

Section 1: Retirement Planning

Importance of Retirement Planning
- Emphasizing the need to plan for financial independence during retirement.
- Addressing the changing landscape of retirement benefits and social security.

Types of Retirement Savings Accounts
- 401(k), IRA, Roth IRA, and other retirement accounts.
- Exploring tax advantages, contribution limits, and withdrawal rules.

Calculating Retirement Needs
- Estimating the amount required for a comfortable retirement lifestyle.
- Factoring in living expenses, healthcare costs, and inflation.

Creating a Retirement Savings Strategy
- Setting specific retirement goals and milestones.
- Diversifying investments and adjusting the portfolio as retirement approaches.

Section 2: Estate Planning

Understanding Estate Planning
- Defining estate planning and its role in managing your assets after death.
- Emphasizing the importance of avoiding probate and minimizing estate taxes.

Creating a Will
- Drafting a legitimately restricting record illustrating the dispersion of your resources.
- Naming an executor to manage your estate and guardians for minor children.

Trusts and Estate Distribution
- Differentiating between revocable and irrevocable trusts.
- Utilizing trusts to ensure asset distribution according to your wishes.

Minimizing Estate Taxes

- Exploring strategies to minimize estate taxes and maximize inheritance for beneficiaries.
- Gifting strategies and tax-efficient methods for passing on wealth.

Section 3: Securing Your Legacy

Naming Beneficiaries

- Refreshing recipient assignments on retirement records and extra security strategies.
- Ensuring your assets pass to the intended recipients smoothly.

Health Care and End-of-Life Directives

- Creating advance directives for healthcare decisions if you become incapacitated.
- Outlining your wishes for medical treatment and life-sustaining measures.

Regularly Reviewing Your Plan

- Recognizing the importance of revisiting your estate plan after life events (marriage, birth, etc.).

- Keeping your plan up-to-date with changing financial and family circumstances.

Seeking Professional Advice
- Consulting with estate planning attorneys, financial advisors, and tax professionals.
- Collaborating to create a comprehensive plan that aligns with your goals.

By immersing yourself in the details outlined within this chapter, you'll gain a comprehensive understanding of retirement and estate planning. This knowledge will empower you to secure your financial future, ensure the smooth transfer of your assets, and leave a lasting legacy for your loved ones.

Appendix A: Present and Future Value Tables

Appendix A provides valuable tables that assist in calculating the present value and future value of investments or cash flows. These tables are essential tools for financial planning, helping individuals make informed decisions about investments, loans, and other financial transactions.

Section 1: Present Value Tables

Understanding Present Value
- Present value is the concept that the value of money today is worth more than the same amount in the future due to factors like inflation and opportunity cost.

Using Present Value Tables
- Present value tables provide a quick reference to calculate the present value of future cash flows.
- By inputting the interest rate and time period, you can determine the present value of a future sum of money.

Section 2: Future Value Tables

Understanding Future Value
- Future value represents the worth of an investment or cash flow at a future date, taking into account interest or growth.

Using Future Value Tables
- Future value tables help estimate the value of an investment over time.
- By inputting the interest rate and time period, you can determine the future value of a present sum of money.

Section 3: Application and Benefits

Investment Decision-Making
- Present and future value tables aid in comparing investment options by quantifying the value of money over time.
- Helps in evaluating the potential returns of different investment choices.

Loan and Mortgage Planning
- Permits borrowers to think about various advance choices and loan fees.
- Allows borrowers to compare different loan options and interest rates.

Retirement Planning

- Calculating the future value of retirement savings helps individuals determine whether they are on track to meet their financial goals.
- Helps in making informed decisions about retirement contributions and investment strategies.

Time Value of Money Concept

- The tables reinforce the time value of money concept, showing how money's value changes over time due to interest, inflation, and opportunity cost.

Section 4: Online and Digital Tools

Digital Calculators and Software

- Present and future value calculations can also be performed using online calculators, financial software, or spreadsheets.
- Provides greater flexibility and precision compared to manual table calculations.

Limitations of Tables

- Tables offer a simplified approach to calculations but may not account for all variables, such as changing interest rates.

By referring to the details provided in this appendix, you'll be equipped with the knowledge to use present and future value tables effectively. These tools will prove invaluable in various financial scenarios, enabling you to make accurate assessments of investment decisions, loans, and savings strategies.

Appendix B: Estimating Social Security Benefits

Appendix B offers a comprehensive guide to estimating Social Security benefits, a crucial component of retirement planning. Understanding how Social Security benefits are calculated empowers individuals to make informed decisions about retirement income and financial security.

Section 1: Basics of Social Security

Importance of Social Security
- Social Security provides a safety net for retirees, disabled individuals, and survivors.
- Understanding the role of Social Security in retirement income planning.

Benefit Eligibility
- Exploring the eligibility criteria for Social Security benefits based on age and work history.
- Understanding the quarters of coverage required for benefit eligibility.

Section 2: Estimating Social Security Benefits

Primary Insurance Amount (PIA)
- Understanding PIA as the baseline benefit amount individuals are entitled to at full retirement age.
- Factors influencing PIA, including average indexed monthly earnings and bend points.

Full Retirement Age
- Identifying the full retirement age based on birth year.
- The impact of claiming benefits before or after full retirement age on benefit amounts.

Early and Delayed Retirement
- Exploring the option to claim benefits as early as age 62 or delay until age 70 for increased benefits.
- The effect of early or delayed retirement on benefit reductions or credits.

Section 3: Special Circumstances

Spousal and Survivor Benefits
- Exploring benefits available to spouses and survivors of eligible workers.
- How spousal benefits can be based on the worker's benefit amount or their own work history.

Working While Receiving Benefits
- Understanding how working while receiving Social Security benefits can impact benefit amounts.
- Exploring the earnings limit and potential reduction in benefits for individuals under full retirement age.

Section 4: Calculators and Online Tools

Social Security Administration's Online Tools
- The Social Security Administration provides online calculators to estimate benefit amounts based on different claiming strategies.
- Calculators help individuals explore various scenarios and make informed decisions.

Limitations and Considerations

- Recognizing that Social Security estimators provide estimates and not exact benefit amounts.
- Considering other sources of retirement income and expenses in retirement planning.

By alluding to the subtleties gave in this reference section, you'll be furnished with the information to gauge your Federal retirement aide benefits actually. This understanding will engage you to make arrangements for retirement pay, settle on informed conclusions about guaranteeing methodologies, and guarantee a monetarily secure retirement.

Glossary

The glossary serves as a comprehensive reference guide to key terms and concepts used throughout the book. Understanding these terms will enhance your comprehension of personal finance, investing, and other financial topics covered in the chapters.

A

- **Asset Allocation:** The process of distributing investments across different asset classes (e.g., stocks, bonds, real estate) to manage risk and achieve specific financial goals.
- **Bonds:** Debt securities issued by governments or corporations, representing a loan made by an investor to the issuer in exchange for periodic interest payments and the return of the bond's face value upon maturity.

C

- **Compound Interest:** A premium that is determined on both the underlying measure of cash (head) and the amassed revenue from past periods.

- **Diversification:** Spreading investments across different assets to reduce risk by minimizing the impact of poor performance in any one investment.

E

- **Equity:** Ownership in a company represented by shares of stock, allowing investors to potentially benefit from the company's growth and profits.
- **Estate Planning:** The process of arranging for the management and distribution of your assets after your death, including the creation of wills, trusts, and beneficiary designations.

F

- **Fixed Income:** Investments that provide a steady stream of income, such as bonds or certificates of deposit.
- **Future Value:** The value of an investment or cash flow at a specified future date, accounting for interest or growth over time.

I

- **Inflation:** The general increase in prices of goods and services over time, reducing the purchasing power of money.
- **Investment Horizon:** The length of time an investor plans to hold an investment before selling or cashing in.

M

- **Mutual Funds:** Pooled funds from multiple investors used to invest in a diversified portfolio of securities, managed by professional fund managers.

P

- **Present Value:** The current value of a future sum of money, taking into account the time value of money.
- **Risk Tolerance:** An individual's ability and willingness to take on risk in their investment choices.

R

- **Retirement Planning:** The process of setting financial goals and strategies to ensure a comfortable retirement, often involving retirement accounts, savings, and investments.
- **Risk and Return:** The principle that greater potential returns are usually associated with greater levels of risk in investment decisions.

S

- **Social Security:** A government program providing financial support to retirees, disabled individuals, and survivors through monthly benefits.

T

- **Tax-Advantaged Accounts:** Accounts like IRAs and 401(k)s that offer tax benefits to encourage retirement savings.
- **Time Value of Money:** The concept that the value of money changes over time due to factors such as interest, inflation, and opportunity cost.

U

- **Uniform Transfers to Minors Act (UTMA):** A legal arrangement allowing adults to gift assets to minors without establishing a trust.
- **Underwriting:** The process of assessing the risk of insuring a person or asset and determining the appropriate insurance premium.

This glossary serves as a quick reference to clarify terms encountered throughout the book, helping you navigate and understand the complex world of personal finance and investment concepts.

Index

The index is a valuable reference tool that provides an organized and comprehensive list of keywords, concepts, and page references found within the book. It enables quick and efficient navigation, making it easier to locate specific information and topics throughout the text.

The index allows you to quickly locate specific terms and concepts mentioned in the book, facilitating efficient information retrieval and enhancing your understanding of the various financial topics covered. Use this index as your guide to navigating the content and finding the information you need.